Rc Lay Eggs

Katie Smythe

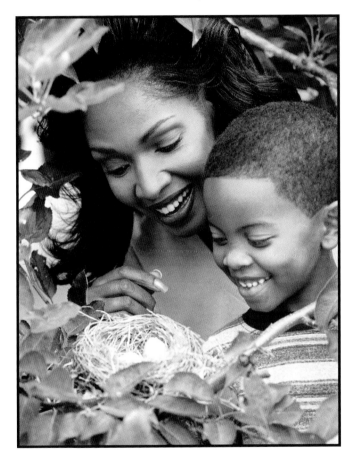

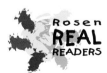

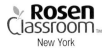

New York

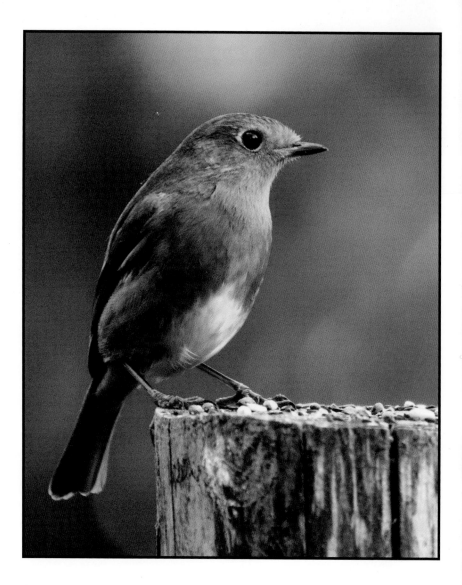

This is a robin.

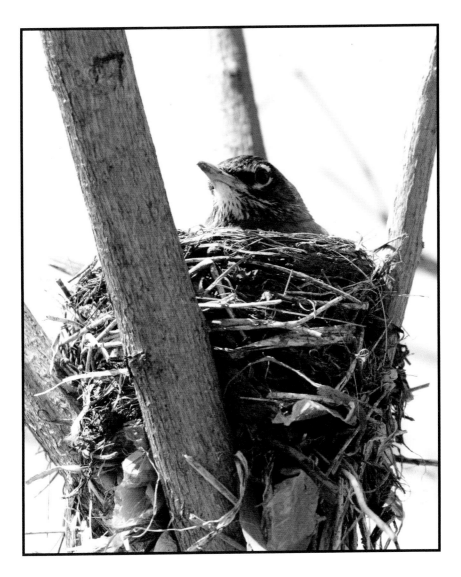

Robins make nests.

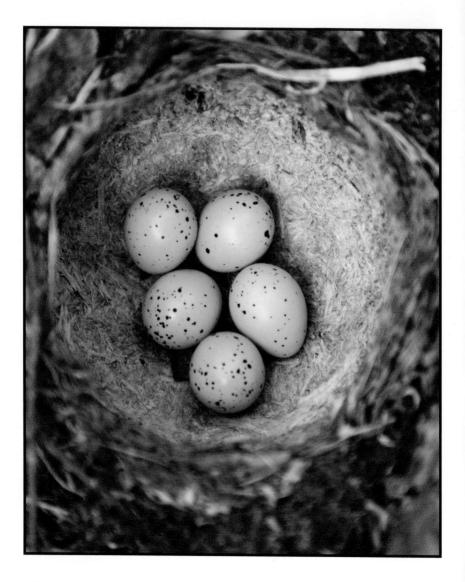

Robins lay blue eggs.

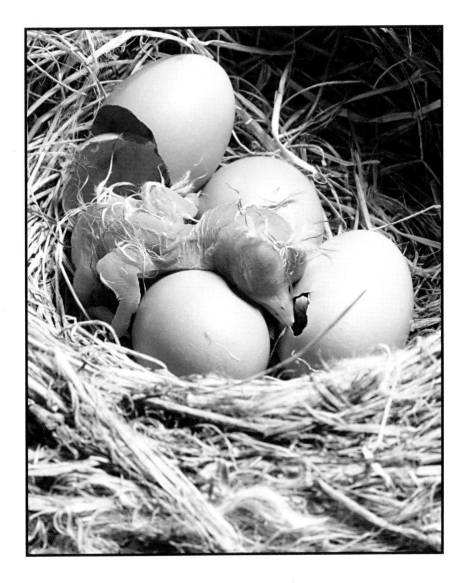

The eggs hatch chicks.

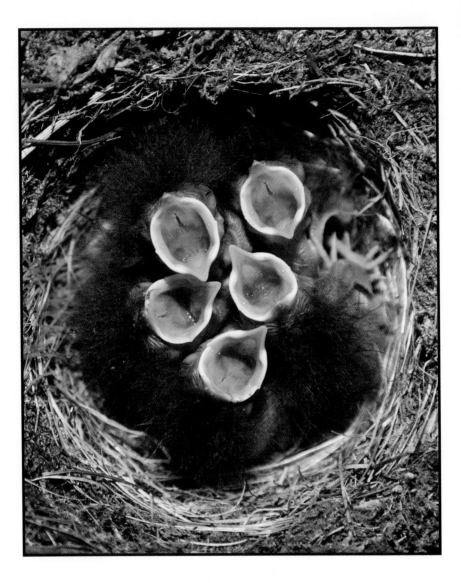

Chicks are baby birds.

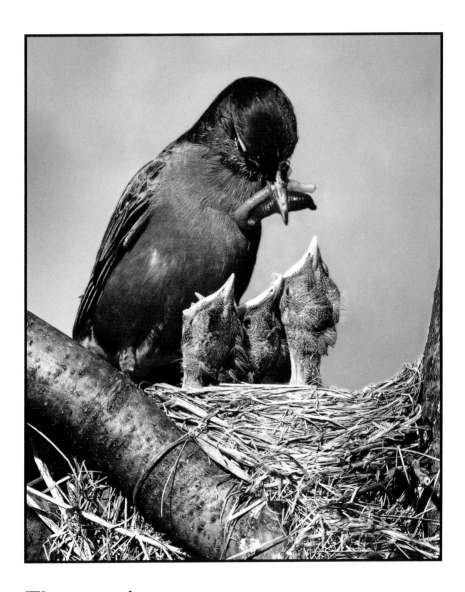

They eat worms.

Words To Know

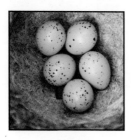

eggs

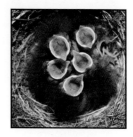

chicks

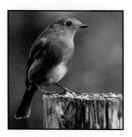

robin

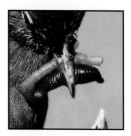

worm